W9-BBW-511

WESTMINSTER SCHOOLS

Lila Katherine

SMYTHE
GAMBRELL
LIBRARY

PRESENTED BY

Meredith Davies
1990

A New True Book

RADIATION

By Dennis Fradin

Consultant: Cary Davids, Ph.D.
Argonne National Laboratory

CHILDRENS PRESS ®

CHICAGO

Radioactive warning sign

PHOTO CREDITS

© Cameramann International, Ltd.—11, 13 (2 photos)
31 (left), 33, 39 (left), 41

EKM-Nepenthe: © Robert Ginn—14 (left)

Journalism Services:
© H. Rick Bamman—8
© Joseph Jacobson—4
© H. J. Prezkop—23

© Photri—6 (right), 7, 27 (right), 31 (right), 39 (right)

© H. Armstrong Roberts—14 (right), 21, 45

© H. Armstrong Roberts/Camerique—Cover

Courtesy Sandia Laboratories—19

Tom Stack & Associates:
© David M. Doody—2, 43
© Stewart M. Green—12

Wide World, Inc.—6 (left), 25, 27 (left), 28, 29, 32, 35
(2 photos), 36 (2 photos)

John Forsberg—16

Cover: Patient in CAT scan

Library of Congress Cataloging-in-Publication Data

Fradin, Dennis B.
  Radiation.

  (A New true book)
  Includes index.
  Summary: Describes what radiation is, its sources and
uses, and the dangers of radiation exposure from nuclear
bombs and power plant leaks.
    1. Radiation—Juvenile literature. [1. Radiation]
I. Title.
QC475.25.F73 1987   539.2   86-30963
ISBN 0-516-01238-X

TABLE OF CONTENTS

Radiation from the sun heats and lights our earth.

WHAT IS RADIATION?

The word *radiation* comes from a Latin word meaning *ray*. Radiation can be defined as energy that moves in the form of waves or particles.

We are surrounded by many kinds of radiation, much of it helpful. Radiation from the sun heats and lights our earth. Without radiation we would have no radio, television, X-rays, or microwave ovens.

Two views of the mushroom cloud resulting from an atomic bomb explosion

Radiation can be harmful, too. Atomic bomb radiation has killed thousands of people. Too much exposure to the sun's rays can cause skin cancer.

Microwave ovens cook food quickly.

RADIATION WAVES AND PARTICLES

Radiation takes two forms—waves and particles. The waves move like ocean waves, only much faster. X-rays, radio waves, and microwaves are three kinds of radiation that move as waves.

Mobile television crews send pictures and sounds
back to the station using microwave guns.

The length of the wave
(called the *wavelength*)
determines the type of
radiation that is produced.
Waves that are about
twenty-five millionths of an
inch long take the form of

visible light. The radio waves that carry AM programs are each several hundred feet long.

Some radiation takes the form of particles much too small to be seen with our eyes. Radiation from atomic bombs is made up of such tiny particles. Cosmic rays, a type of radiation given off by the sun and other stars, also are tiny particles.

NATURAL VERSUS MAN-MADE RADIATION

Much of the radiation we are exposed to occurs naturally. Since it is always present, it is called *background radiation.* Cosmic rays and the sun's heat and light are main types of background radiation.

Background radiation is generally too weak to hurt living things. For example,

Too much exposure to the sun and its ultraviolet rays can harm humans.

hundreds of cosmic rays strike us each minute without harming us. Some types of background radiation are dangerous in large doses, however. Long exposure to the sun's ultraviolet rays causes most skin cancers.

Among the other forms of radiation that occur in nature are X-rays, radio waves, and nuclear radiation. Stars emit these three types of radiation. People have learned to produce these types of radiation, too.

This CAT scanner is used to see inside a patient's skull.

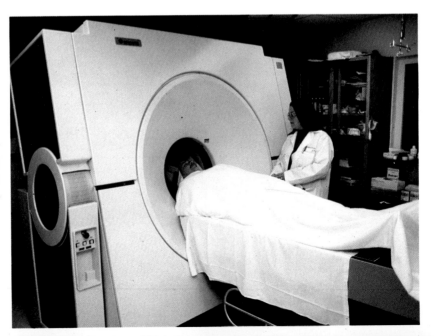

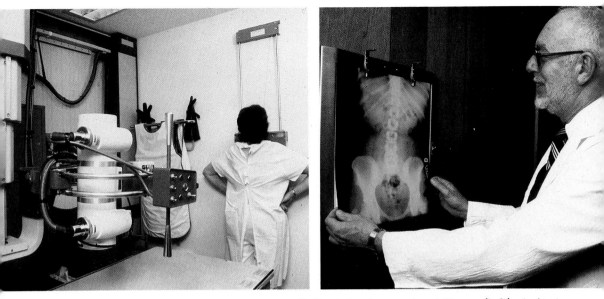

Patient having a chest X-ray (left). A doctor
checks an X-ray (right).

Doctors use X-rays when
they want to see inside
our bodies. Since X-rays
tend to kill abnormal cells,
they are also used to fight
cancer. Each time we turn
on the radio or TV we
make use of radio waves.

13

Diablo Canyon (left) and the Maine Yankee nuclear plant (right) use nuclear energy to supply electricity to their customers.

Nuclear radiation is a very dangerous form of man-made radiation. It is produced by bombs and power plants that are fueled by nuclear energy.

WHAT IS NUCLEAR ENERGY?

To understand nuclear energy, you must know a little about *atoms*—the tiny units that make up matter. Everything in the universe is made of atoms. Atoms are so small that millions of them can fit on the point of a pin.

There are three main kinds of particles in atoms: *protons*, *neutrons*,

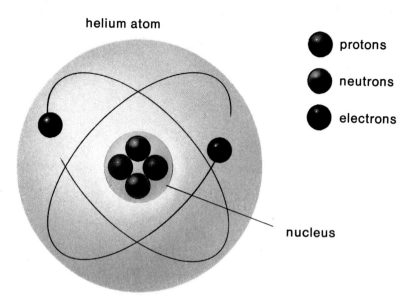

helium atom

protons

neutrons

electrons

nucleus

and *electrons*. Protons and
neutrons are found in the
cores of atoms. An atom's
core is called the *nucleus*
(plural *nuclei*). The
electrons are located
outside the nucleus.

The forces that hold

protons and neutrons together in the nuclei possess a lot of energy. Sometimes some of that energy escapes from the nuclei. Energy that comes from the nuclei of atoms is called *nuclear energy.*

There are two ways that scientists produce nuclear energy. One way is to split atoms into pieces, releasing the energy. Splitting atoms to release energy is called *nuclear fission*. Atomic bombs and nuclear reactors work by fission.

The other way that scientists unleash nuclear energy is called *nuclear fusion*. This involves fusing (joining together) nuclei. As this occurs, some of the matter is turned into energy and escapes from the nuclei. The most powerful weapon ever built, the hydrogen bomb, works by nuclear fusion.

THE DANGERS OF NUCLEAR RADIATION

In a nuclear reaction, energy in the form of heat is given off, and used to generate electricity. Materials that give off *nuclear radiation* are also produced. These materials are said to be *radioactive*.

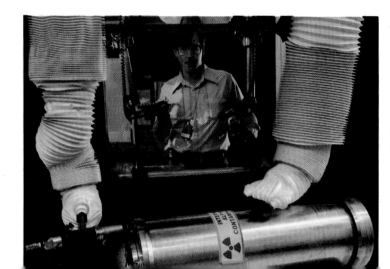

Robot arms are used to handle radioactive containers. Do you see the radioactive warning sign on the container?

Nuclear radiation comes in three forms. They are called *alpha particles*, *beta particles*, and *gamma rays*. An alpha particle consists of two protons and two neutrons. A beta particle is an electron. Gamma rays are waves that are similar to X-rays.

There are several constructive uses for nuclear radiation. Doctors sometimes use radioactive materials to treat cancer.

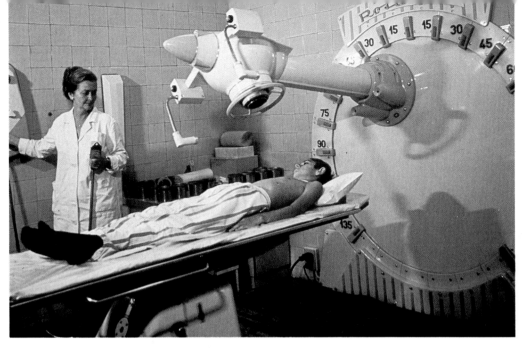

Cancer patient receives radiation treatments
to kill or stop the growth of cancer cells.

But in large quantities
nuclear radiation harms
the cells of the body. As a
result, the cells cannot do
their jobs. The person gets
sick and may even die.
Illness caused by radiation
is called *radiation sickness*.

21

The amount of radiation a person receives is measured in *rems*. Background radiation exposes a person to less than one-tenth of a rem per year. A single dose of 100 rems can bring on radiation sickness. A 300-rem dose will make a person very sick. One thousand rems will bring on death.

The biggest problem in discovering the presence

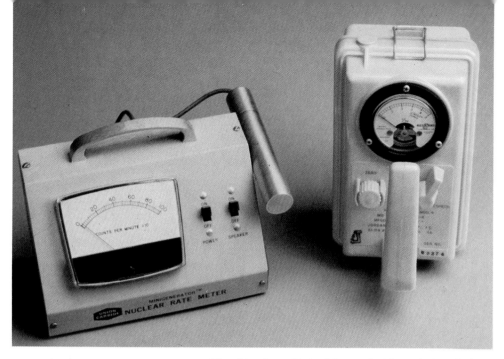

The Nuclear Rate Meter (left) and the Geiger counter (right) measure amounts of radiation.

of nuclear radiation is that people cannot feel, taste, hear, smell, or see it. Geiger counters and other devices must be used to measure radiation in an area.

RADIATION DISASTERS FROM BOMBS

There have been several radiation disasters in the short time that people have used nuclear energy. The two worst came in the form of bombs that were dropped on Japan.

During World War II (1939–1945) the United States built a new weapon—the atomic bomb, or A-bomb. Its fuel was the element uranium. To

Artist's drawing shows the team of scientists under the direction of Dr. Enrico Fermi conducting the first chain reaction in the world's first nuclear reactor on December 2, 1942. All tests were done in secret. No photographers or reporters were allowed to observe this historic event.

explode the A-bomb, first some uranium nuclei were split by shooting some neutrons at them. More neutrons released from the broken uranium nuclei then split other uranium nuclei. The result was a *chain reaction* in which trillions of uranium nuclei were split, causing a huge explosion

In 1945 the United States decided that the war would end faster if atomic bombs were dropped on Japan. On August 6, 1945, a U.S. plane dropped an A-bomb on Hiroshima, Japan. About

The actual photograph of the atomic bomb hitting the city of Nagasaki on August 9, 1945 (left), and the ruins of Nagasaki after the blast (right)

100,000 people died in the blast. Three days later the U.S. dropped an A-bomb on Nagasaki, Japan. This time about 40,000 people died.

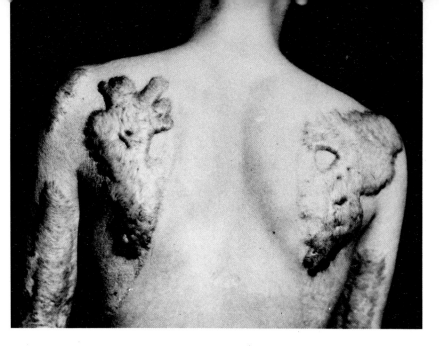

Scarred body of a survivor of the atomic bomb explosion at Hiroshima.

The two A-bombs dropped on Japan killed people in several ways. The spots where the bombs exploded were as hot as the sun for an instant. Thousands of people within a few blocks of the blasts were burned

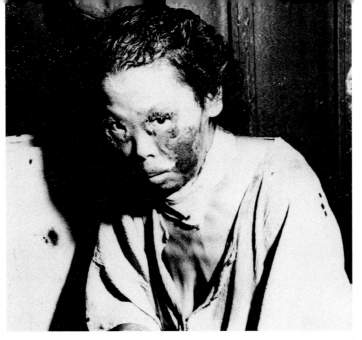

Many burn victims later died of illnesses caused by radiation released by the atomic bomb.

to death. Thousands who survived the heat were killed very quickly by the radiation. Many others who were a mile or so away seemed fine for a while, but then died days later from the radiation that had poisoned their bodies.

The A-bombs that rocked Japan were still killing people years later. People who receive large radiation doses are prone to cancer. Due to A-bomb radiation, thousands of people at Hiroshima and Nagasaki died of cancer many years after the blasts.

During the early 1950s, the United States built a much more powerful nuclear bomb. It was called the *hydrogen bomb*,

In Hiroshima Peace Park (left) the skeleton of the building over which the atom bomb was dropped stands as a grim reminder of the destructive power of the bomb. The hydrogen bomb (right) is much more powerful than the atomic bomb.

or *H-bomb*. At that time the United States was testing many hydrogen bombs. The tests produced a lot of *fallout*. Fallout consists of dangerous radioactive materials that fall slowly to earth after a nuclear explosion. Due to the fallout, people who were in the blast areas developed more cases of

cancer than was normal. This is one reason why most nations now test their nuclear weapons underground.

A plume of smoke rises from an underground nuclear explosion.

Control
room at a
nuclear
power plant

NUCLEAR REACTOR RADIATION LEAKS

While nuclear bombs
were constructed, some
peaceful uses for nuclear
energy were found as well.
Nuclear reactors were

built. These are machines which split uranium nuclei to create electric power. Many nations built nuclear reactors during the 1950s through the 1980s. Today 400 nuclear power plants produce one-sixth of the world's electricity.

Nuclear power plants pollute the air less than plants that use coal or oil to produce electricity. But nuclear power plants have one big problem.

Damaged buildings at Chernobyl nuclear power station (left). Medical technician (right) checks the radiation levels of some of the people exposed to radiation because of the accident at Chernobyl.

Radiation sometimes leaks from them.

There have been many small radiation leaks at nuclear power plants, and several large ones. One major leak occurred in 1986 at the Chernobyl

Radiation from Chernobyl was carried by the wind to all
parts of Europe. A West German fireman (above) scrubs
down a car discovered to be carrying radioactive dirt.
Aerial view of the Three Mile Island nuclear plant
in Pennsylvania (right)

Nuclear Power Plant in
Russia. Several dozen
people near the power
plant died from radiation
sickness within days of

the accident. Thousands more may one day develop cancer due to the radiation they received.

The worst U.S. nuclear power plant leak occurred in 1979 at the Three Mile Island nuclear reactor in Pennsylvania. Fortunately, the problem was solved minutes before a huge amount of radiation would have been released, so no one died in the Three Mile Island accident.

THE PROBLEMS OF RADIOACTIVE WASTES

In 1957 some nuclear wastes buried in Russia's Ural Mountains mysteriously exploded, perhaps by overheating their containers. Vast amounts of radiation rose into the air. Dozens of people are thought to have died. At least a dozen villages were wiped off the map, because they were

Strong, lead-lined containers
are used to store radioactive
materials that are no longer in use.

too "hot" (radioactive) to
allow people to remain
living there.

This disaster points out
another problem with
nuclear energy. Radioactive
wastes are created along
with the energy. These

wastes cannot be thrown away like garbage, because some of them stay radioactive for thousands of years. A person who found them could die of radiation sickness.

Many nuclear wastes now are being kept in special tanks in the power plants. But this solves the problem just for today. Places must be found where no one will ever disturb the radioactive

These radioactive fuel rods can no longer be used. They are stored under water at a General Electric storage facility in Illinois.

wastes. The United States has a plan, which should go into effect in the late 1990s, to store large amounts of nuclear wastes underground. The U.S. nuclear dump will be carefully maintained and guarded. Some people think that one day nuclear wastes may also be placed beneath the ocean floor.

Another problem is that nuclear reactors last only about fifty years. Around the year 2000 reactors built in the 1950s and 1960s will be closed down. Since they will contain lots of radiation, the old plants will not be knocked down but may have to be taken apart and buried in spots where no one will ever find them.

A worker checks radiation levels outside a nuclear power plant.

A GREAT THREAT TO HUMANITY

Many people think that the possibility of uncontrolled release of nuclear radiation is the greatest threat facing humanity. A radiation leak

from a nuclear reactor
could kill many thousands
of people. Radiation from
a nuclear war could kill
every last person on earth.

We benefit from the use
of nuclear energy, and as
a result we are faced with
several big challenges.
People must never again
drop a nuclear bomb on
other people. We must
make sure that all nuclear
power plants are as safe
as possible. We must see

to it that nuclear wastes
are disposed of safely.
Human beings have no
choice about answering
these challenges. We don't
want to have more
Hiroshimas and Chernobyls
in our future, do we?

WORDS YOU SHOULD KNOW

alpha particle(AL • fa PAR • tih • kil) — a particle, emitted by radioactive nuclei, which consists of two protons and two neutrons

atomic bomb(ah • TOM • ik BAHMB) — a powerful bomb which works by nuclear fission

atoms(AT • umz) — very tiny units that make up matter

background radiation(BACK • ground ray • dee • AISH • un) — natural radiation which is always present

beta particle(BAY • ta PAR • tih • kil) — an electron, emitted by radioactive nuclei

cancer(KAN • ser) — a disease in which atypical cells multiply wildly

chain reaction(CHAYNE re • AK • shun) — a process which keeps going by itself

cosmic rays(kahz • mik • RAIZ) — radiation particles given off by the sun and other stars

electron(e • LEK • trahn) — a particle which orbits an atom's nucleus

fallout(FAWL • out) — dangerous radioactive materials that fall slowly to earth after the explosion of a nuclear bomb

gamma rays(GAM • ah • RAIZ) — powerful radiation waves that are similar to X-rays

Geiger counter(GUY • ger COWN • ter) — a device used to detect and measure radiation

hydrogen bomb(HYE • dru • gin BOMB) — a nuclear fusion bomb which is the most powerful weapon ever built

microwaves(MY • kro • waivz) — short radio waves

million(MIL • yun) — a thousand thousand (1,000,000)

neutron(NOO • tron) — a particle found in the nucleus of an atom

nuclear energy(NOO • klee • er EN • er • gy) — energy produced by changes in the nuclei of atoms

nuclear fission(NOO • klee • er FISH • un)—a process by which nuclei of atoms are split, releasing tremendous energy

nuclear fusion(NOO • klee • er FYOO • zjun)—a process in which nuclei of atoms join together, releasing tremendous energy

nuclear power plants(NOO • klee • er POW • er PLANTZ)—buildings where electricity is produced from nuclear energy

nuclear radiation(NOO • klee • er ray • dee • A • shun)—the energy given off by the nuclei of atoms in the form of waves or particles. It is harmful in large quantities.

nuclear reactors(NOO • klee • er ree • ACK • terz)—machines which split atomic nuclei to produce electricity

nucleus (of an atom)(NOO • klee • us)—the center of the atom where the protons and neutrons are located

proton(PRO • tahn)—a particle which is found in the nucleus of an atom

radiation(ray • dee • A • shun)—energy that moves in the form of waves or particles

radiation sickness(ray • dee • A • shun SIK • niss)—illness caused by a large dose of nuclear radiation

radioactivity(ray • dee • oh • ack • TIHV • ih • tee)—the process of giving off radiation

rem(REM)—a unit used to measure radiation received by a person

uranium(you • RAY • nee • um)—an element which is the main fuel used to create nuclear fission

wavelength(WAIV • length)—the length of an individual wave

X-rays(X • raiz)—a kind of radiation used by doctors to see inside the body

INDEX

About the author

*Dennis Fradin attended Northwestern University on a partial
creative scholarship and graduated in 1967. His previous books
include the Young People's Stories of Our States series for
Childrens Press, and Bad Luck Tony for Prentice-Hall. In the True
book series Dennis has written about astronomy, farming, comets,
archaeology, movies, space colonies, the space lab, explorers, and
pioneers. He is married and the father of three children.*